HACKING LITERACY

HACKING
LITERACY

5 Ways To Turn Any Classroom
Into a Culture of Readers

Gerard Dawson

PUBLICATIONS

Hacking Literacy
© 2016 by Times 10 Publications

These books are available at special discounts when purchased in quantity for use as premiums, promotions, fundraising, and educational use. For inquiries and details, contact us at www.hacklearning.org.

Published by Times 10
Cleveland, OH
HackLearning.org

Cover Design by Tracey Henterly
Interior Design by Steven Plummer
Editing by Ruth Arseneault
Proofreading by Jennifer Jas

Library of Congress Control Number: 2016946078
ISBN: 978-0-9861049-5-4
First Printing: August, 2016

TABLE OF CONTENTS

PUBLISHER'S FOREWORD

MOST EDUCATORS WHO know my work think of me as the blogger who wants to throw out grades, or the teacher who hates homework, or simply as the Hack Learning guy. While each of these descriptions is accurate to one degree or another, what few people know is that I am most passionate about literacy. I believe that if all students loved books and became avid readers, every single aspect of education that we attempt to measure would improve. Test scores would skyrocket. Learners would excel in every area of interest. Participation in co-curricular activities and community service would increase. All students would graduate. Poverty and crime might eventually disappear, and our prisons would become empty shells.

If even one of these bold beliefs is true, one would think that every educator's primary goal would be to foster the love of reading. How is it, then, that our schools fall so dreadfully short when it comes to producing literate students? One answer, and this is my own hypothesis based on more than two decades as a classroom teacher, is that the entire structure of school is designed to inhibit literacy. Because we focus on standards, competency, and high stakes test scores, encouraging a love of reading, writing, and of books is rarely assigned the importance that it deserves.

Enter Gerard Dawson, an education hacker who grasps the one simple idea that eludes so many new and veteran teachers: When students learn to love reading, everything else we work so relentlessly to teach falls seamlessly into place. Not only does Dawson understand this notion, he has built a classroom that gives action to the idea, spawning a beautiful, vibrant culture of readers.

In *Hacking Literacy*, the sixth book in the *Hack Learning Series*, Dawson reveals the characteristics of this culture and shares the simple strategies that empower any teacher to replicate it. Along the way, Dawson identifies problems that educators face as they attempt to teach often-reluctant learners to read and write daily, and he provides examples and anecdotes from other educators who have built their own reading cultures.

Education hackers like Gerard Dawson are tinkerers and fixers. As with all hackers, they see solutions to problems that other people do not see. They are specialists who grapple with issues that need to be turned upside down or viewed with a different lens. The fixes they suggest may appear unusual at first, but as each chapter unfolds, their purposes will become clear and you'll be as eager as you've ever been to implement them immediately in your own classroom and school.

INSIDE THE BOOKS

Each book in the series contains chapters, called Hacks, which are composed of these sections:

- **The Problem:** Something educators are currently wrestling with that doesn't appear to have a clear solution.

- **The Hack:** A brief description of the author's unique fix.

- **What You Can Do Tomorrow:** Ways you can take the basic hack and implement it right away in bare-bones form.

- **Blueprint for Full Implementation:** A step-by-step system for building long-term capacity.

- **Overcoming Pushback:** A list of possible objections you might come up against in your attempt to implement this hack and how to overcome each one.

- **The Hack in Action:** A snapshot of an educator or group of educators who have used this hack in their work and how they did it.

I am proud to be the publisher of and a contributing author to the *Hack Learning Series*, which is changing how we view and solve problems in teaching and learning. When you finish reading this book, you will understand the simplicity of building a culture of readers. You may begin to see solutions to other problems that you've previously overlooked. In the end, you might even become an education hacker.

And that's a good thing.

—*MARK BARNES, EDUCATION HACKER AND AVID READER*

INTRODUCTION

*If you always do what you've always done, you'll
always get what you've always gotten.*

—JESSIE POTTER, DIRECTOR OF THE NATIONAL INSTITUTE FOR HUMAN RELATIONSHIPS

IMAGINE A CLASSROOM centered around a culture of readers. In such an environment, reading is celebrated instead of just being assessed. When the focus shifts away from grades to honor the pleasures of learning, students take ownership of their reading lives. They cultivate the habits that develop lifelong readers.

Students whose teachers facilitate a culture of reading engage actively in reading. They submerge themselves in books, perhaps leaving their desks to lounge in comfortable spots on the floor, and drift mentally away from their immediate environment. Because they recognize the personal benefits of finding terrific reads, they use a variety of channels to seek out new books. They talk to other students about books they love or loathe, they recommend books to their friends, they search recommendation lists online and add books to their "To Read" lists. Anyone who finishes a book discusses it with the teacher or tells the whole class about it. Other students listen, hoping to find their next great read. The students set their own goals for reading, keep track of books they've read, and write about their reading in meaningful ways.

Some teachers might argue that creating a culture of readers is a waste of time: Teachers are required to follow a literature curriculum. In response to this concern, I'd like to pose a question: Is the study of whole class texts and literature worthwhile if the cost is the death of reading? When we focus on coverage, assessing students' ability to parrot back facts and ideas that they have gleaned from class discussions—or the Internet—rather than their own responses to texts, we create the illusion that kids are actually engaging in reading. Too many of America's students pass through their upper elementary, middle, and high school educations never reading a book cover to cover.

I aim to create a culture of reading with my students. Unlike some clear milestones in education—completing a course, being hired for a new position, helping a child move on to the next grade—this goal has no fixed end point. The process is the purpose. Teachers who create a culture of reading consistently reinforce a mindset, system, and set of habits that draw students into rich lives as literate citizens.

This book will not outline a systematic process to implement precisely. Instead, we'll explore practices designed to solve a literacy teacher's most common concern: How do I inspire students to read often and read well?

I don't claim to have experience or knowledge that others don't have. This book is not about me, a high school English and journalism teacher who's in his fifth year of teaching. Rather, it's a distillation of all of the conversations, professional books, presentations, and classroom experiences I've processed, broken down into five actionable steps.

Because the ideas in this book are called hacks, you might think that these fixes are *easy* fixes. *Simple* fixes is more accurate. Building a culture of readers is not easy: It takes time, patience, and consistent application of effective strategies. Luckily, the most effective strategies I have found are simple ones without too many moving parts.

The five hacks that follow adopt a student-centered perspective on student literacy. They're founded in the notion that individuals become better readers when they are engaged, active members of a culture that values reading. Nurturing this culture of reading involves finding the best practices to develop and refine student literacy, adjusting the way you implement these practices for your particular situation as you move forward, and continually seeking ways to improve.

In his book *Power and Portfolios: Best Practices for High School Classrooms*, my mentor Jim Mahoney maintains that school is all about power: who has it, who wants it, and what they're going to do once they get it. His insight illuminates a central shift in attitude that we must undertake if a healthy classroom culture is to be nurtured. We must expose the reality of the unspoken struggle for power in classrooms, which typically delimits the sort of changes that teachers are willing (or able) to implement. Building a culture of readers involves taking the risk of ceding power to the students. It means empowering students to manage their own learning and measure their own progress. As the teacher releases rigid control and invites students to collaborate in building a culture of readers, the energy of the classroom transforms itself.

The hacks in this book will encourage teachers to discontinue ineffective practices such as:

- Falling back on multiple choice quizzes, reading checks, and homework grades to force students into reading,

- Lecturing students about the "true meaning" of a classic work of literature,

- Assigning writing and speaking tasks that students can complete based on SparkNotes and the ideas of their classmates.

The *Hack in Action* sections will introduce you to superb teachers who will inspire you to:

- Cultivate an environment where students want to read,

- Share your own reading life with your students,

- Facilitate authentic writing and speaking about reading,

- Allot sustained periods of time for students to read in class.

A computer hacker finds simple but elegant solutions to complex problems that those who are limited by traditional perspectives cannot see. *Hacking Literacy* offers you five simple hacks to transform your thinking and your language arts classroom.

HACK 1

FOCUS ON THE READER

There are only two ways to influence human behavior:
You can manipulate it or you can inspire it.
—SIMON SINEK, AUTHOR / TED SPEAKER

THE PROBLEM: BUILDING A CULTURE OF READING FEELS OVERWHELMING

WHEN THE PROSPECT of a significant change confronts you, it's easy to fall into the trap of believing the change has to be all or nothing. Thus, a teacher who considers implementing a culture of reading might think either: *My students will engage in deep reading tomorrow,* or *That's not going to work for these kids.* This binary thinking impedes progress. There certainly will be obstacles to confront, but every student deserves the opportunity to participate fully in a culture of reading.

Even if a teacher is willing to start a reading revolution, the goal might seem so daunting that it's difficult to take that first step. Rather than plunging into the unknown, some teachers are tempted to believe that if they do enough planning, if they read another PD book, if they can obtain the right information from another teacher on Twitter, then they'll be ready to transform their reading class-rooms. But that's not the case. Class culture needs to be developed by the participants, not imported into the classroom and imposed upon them. Just as a home is built brick by brick, a classroom of student readers is built student by student, conversation by conversation, book by book.

THE HACK: FOCUS ON THE READER

A culture of reading is founded in students' identities as readers. Teachers must therefore patiently guide students to shape self-images as readers. Begin by learning about students' perceptions of themselves and their attitudes about reading, model for them how to embody reading habits and behaviors, and invest time in making sure that the right books get into each student's hands.

If sustained silent reading has not been a part of your students' experiences of school, avoid rushing into it by asking students to read for long stretches of time. They'll need to build stamina while they get used to choosing their own books and reading in class. This period of acclimatization may feel like a waste of time, but remember that you must grow the reader before focusing on the reading.

Support the students as they find appealing books and then give them a short period of time to read every day. I'm talking small: five to ten minutes. This will whet the appetite of the students who are ready to read, and it will allow you to identify non-readers before they get frustrated and discouraged or disrupt the other kids. Some students will need more support to find books that interest them and to understand why building a culture of reading in the classroom will benefit them. When the reading routine feels established and students are immersed in books, you will be able to loosen the reins and give students more freedom and time to read.

 **WHAT YOU CAN DO TOMORROW**

Take a few of these actions tomorrow to learn about students' reading lives and show them how to be readers:

- **Show students where to find books.** Take students to the school library and explain the layout. I do this with my school librarian, Amy Gazaleh, at the beginning of each year. Many students are unaware of the contents of the library. Show them how to locate books that will interest them, including non-traditional books like graphic novels; point out books about their favorite athletes or celebrities; explain any book displays; make sure they know the library hours and policies. Give kids time to check out books during this visit if possible. This one-time visit yields year-long dividends.

- **Share your reading life with students.** Bring in the book you are reading, hold it up in front of the students, and tell them about it. If you have a Goodreads page, show students your account, point out the "My Books" section, scroll through your "Want to Read" and "Read" lists, and explain your own preferences as a reader. Discuss books that had a profound effect on your development as a reader. This glimpse of your reading identity will build your credibility as a lead learner in your classroom's culture of reading.

- **Conduct a reading survey.** Hand out slips of paper and ask students, *What's the first thing that comes to mind when you hear the word "reading"? Explain your response.* Their answers will supply you with valuable insights to work from as you move forward. If you have more time, you can ask other questions to find out how students see themselves as readers, how their home lives support or discourage reading, and how they feel about their current reading levels. If you're short on time, see this chapter's *Hack in Action* section to learn about the way Jori Krulder uses surveys to empower students and build momentum in her reading classroom.

- **Make "To Read" lists.** When kids who have been non-readers find a book they enjoy and actually finish it, they often end up in a slump because they do not have a new reading selection lined up. In contrast, good readers usually know the next book that they'll be reading long before they close their current read. Have students make "To Read" lists to keep the reading momentum going. Let students decide the location of their list: They might open up to a clean page in a notebook, start a Google Doc, or make a digital note in Evernote or Google Keep. Ask them to write down the titles of any books that they would like to read in the future. If your request receives crickets as a response, there's no need to worry: The rest of this chapter is filled with ideas for inspiring kids' interest in books.

- **Create a class reading record.** You can begin from day one to record observations about who reads consistently and who doesn't, which books students are reading, when they finish books, and even their reasons for choosing certain books. Many wonderful literacy educators, including Nancie Atwell and Penny Kittle, recommend using some version of a "status of the class" report to keep track of student activity on one chart or spreadsheet. You can choose to fill out the status of the class for everyone, or students can take charge of their own entries. The type of comments you include may differ depending on who is recording information. You might include:

  - Book title
  - Genre
  - Current page

- A short comment about progress (for example, "second book in a series," "may be losing interest," "reading a lot at home")
- Whether the book belongs to your classroom, the school library, or the student

Find a piece of paper, or open a new spreadsheet if you prefer to use a mobile device or laptop. To make a spreadsheet, list each student's name in the left-most column, and write dates for the upcoming week along the top of the page. If you're making your chart on paper, devote a new sheet to each week so you have sufficient room to write comments. The document will serve as a place for you to keep track of students' reading habits and record observations from reading conferences. I use a multi-tabbed spreadsheet to collect the rich data from all of my students in one place.

Student Story:

The reading record accumulates in value as the weeks go on. Having a running account of student activity and progress allows the teacher to see trends and patterns that might go unnoticed and that would probably affect student performance in the long run. Earlier this year I noticed that one of my students, Nifferlyn, was engaged in John Green's *Will Grayson, Will Grayson*, but she would often forget to bring the book to class. This became apparent when the reading

---

record showed *Will Grayson, Will Grayson* next to some days and random titles interspersed throughout the weeks. I asked Nifferlyn to set a daily notification using the reminders feature on her phone so she would remember to put her book in her backpack every night. She always had her phone with her, so this easy solution allowed Nifferlyn to read the same book every day. If not for the reading record, it is likely that I would've overlooked her inconsistent preparation.

A BLUEPRINT FOR FULL IMPLEMENTATION

Step 1: Give book talks and present read-alouds.

A book talk is a sales pitch for a book, given by a teacher or student standing in front of the classroom. Bring in a few of your favorite books or ask the school librarian about the current popular titles and borrow a few copies. Talk about the title, the author, the genre, the difficulty level, and anything that may get kids interested in the book. Read the first page or two aloud. At the end, say: *Are you interested in this book? If so, add this to your "To Read" list right now. Again, the title is _____ and the author is _____. You can find this book at _____.* I start the year with daily book talks and then gradually move students toward giving the book talks to each other. See *Hack 4* for more on student book talks.

Step 2: Preview books with a book pass.

When students enter the class, have 1 to 5 books waiting on each desk. Present a mini-lesson on how to preview a book. This is a skill that teachers often overlook when we try to develop lifelong readers.

Experienced readers have internalized processes to determine whether they are interested in a book. Reluctant or inexperienced readers have not yet learned how to do this. They will look at the cover and move on, or choose a book at random and hope for the best. The steps that readers take to analyze a book's appeal need to be made explicit for some students. Show them that they can find an excerpt, summary, or review of the book on the inside flap or back cover.

Read the blurbs from media sources or other authors on the back of the book. Teach students how to read the first page, count the number of unfamiliar words, consider the complexity of the sentences, and make an educated assessment of the book's difficulty level. Readers can also note the feel of the book: Is text big or small? How much white space is on each page? What is the tactile impact of the paper? How lengthy are the paragraphs? The physical impact of the book can add to or detract from the reading experience.

Set students up with a note-taking process for the book pass. I've seen teachers (myself included) get carried away with this. Simple is better. Ask students to record the title, a rating, and a short comment about each book. Leave the rating system up to the students. They can use numbers, stars, smiley/sad faces, or any other symbols that work to represent their evaluation of the books.

Give students a pre-determined amount of time to preview the books on their desks and write down their notes. Call "pass" when time is up and have them pass their books to the right. Repeat the process until all the books have been previewed or until students are getting restless. This process, while engaging and fun, does take some mental energy. Leave enough closure time so that kids have a few minutes to walk around the room and find one book that they might be interested in reading. Follow up with one of these strategies:

- Students add the titles of interesting books to their "To Read" lists.

- Students explain the books that they've retrieved in a think-pair-share format: They jot down a quick note about their selection, share this thinking with a partner, then present their partner's choice to the whole class.

- Students hold up a number of fingers based on how many books they've added to their "To Read" lists.

- Students simply enjoy a few minutes to begin reading their selections.

Step 3: Send kids off on a digital scavenger hunt.

The purpose of the digital scavenger hunt is to show students where they can find and read books online. This will help them grow their "To Read" lists, and it shows them how to look for books at any time with a mobile device. This activity works well as a scavenger hunt because it includes specific tasks for students to complete in a determined sequence. The students bring back artifacts from the scavenger hunt in the form of screenshots, indicating that they've completed the tasks.

Typically, our scavenger hunt includes the following tasks:

A. Access Goodreads.com:

1. Create a Goodreads account.

2. Join the class Goodreads group. (This is not imperative, but it allows students to communicate easily about their reading choices.)

3. Add books to your bookshelf, placing them on "read," "to-read," and "currently-reading" lists.

4. Write a short review of a book you've enjoyed in the past.

5. Find the teacher's account and the school librarian's account and friend them. (Goodreads is fairly devoid of personal information, so many teachers feel comfortable letting their students connect with them on this platform in a way they might not on other platforms, like Facebook, for example.)

B. Search for a book recommendation list that appeals to you, like Time's The 100 Best YA Books of All Time:

1. Skim through the list.

2. Find two to three choices that look interesting.

C. Open Amazon.com:

1. Search for one book you want to read and use the "Look inside" feature to preview it.

2. Look at the "Customers who viewed this item also bought" section to get additional book recommendations.

D. Sign in to the school library's digital catalog:

1. Look up a book that you want to read.

2. Determine if the book is checked out or available.

E. Go to Feedly.com*:

1. Create an account.

2. Click on topics that you are interested in. (The site gives students many options, such as gaming, sports, and fashion.)

3. Find the individual sites or blogs about those topics.

4. Add as many of those sites to your feed as you'd like.

5. Click into an article, preview it, and visit the website where it was originally published.

*Feedly is an online RSS (really simple syndication) reader. When news websites or blogs are updated, an RSS reader automatically takes those updates and posts them in a user's RSS feed. When students set up their Feedly accounts and select topics and sites that interest them, they are creating a personalized nonfiction reading list. Each time they log into Feedly, their feed will be populated by the most recently published articles related to all of the topics they have selected.

To provide evidence that they've accomplished each task, students show the teacher screenshots of their work. For example, when a student makes a Goodreads profile and fills the bookshelf, he or she takes a screenshot of the online bookshelf and adds it to a Google

Doc. The assignment is finished when the student has completed all of the tasks on the scavenger hunt, has taken a screenshot of each task, and has added new books to his or her "To Read" list based on recommendations they have discovered.

Bonus Hack: How to take a screenshot on a few popular devices

> **iPhone/iPad:** Simultaneously press down the lock button at the top of the device and the home button. The photo will appear in your camera roll.
>
> **PC:** Click on the Windows icon at the bottom left of the screen, open the Snipping Tool, and drag the crosshairs around the area of the page you'd like to screenshot. You'll need to save the photo before sharing it or inserting it into a document.
>
> **Mac:** Press Command+Shift+4, then drag the crosshairs around the part of the page you'd like to screenshot. The photo will appear on your desktop.
>
> **Chromebook:** Press Ctrl+Shift+Window Switcher Key (this looks like a rectangle with two lines next to it), then drag the crosshairs around the part of the page you'd like to screenshot. Click "Copy to clipboard," then paste the photo wherever you'd like to view it.

I reinforce this learning throughout the year by modeling how to use the digital tools. At the beginning of a class, I pull up Amazon or Goodreads to show students the book I'm reading. If I've just finished a book, I'll write a short Goodreads review in front of the students. If a student is giving a book talk, I'll pull his or her book up on Amazon, go to the **"Look inside"** section, and either the student or I will read an excerpt from the first page. This reminds students that these tools are available until every student finds a preferred way to manage his or her reading life. I occasionally prompt students to log in to their Feedly accounts and spend the independent reading time perusing nonfiction articles from their feeds.

Step 4: Set a routine and stick to it.

After investing in cultivating students' identities as readers, begin each class with time for reading. Various instructional moves facilitate this routine:

- Subscribe to a service like Remind.com so you can text students reminders about bringing their books to class.

- Find some statistics about the importance of reading (I like the National Endowment for the Arts' report "Reading at Risk: A Survey of Literary Reading in America"). Project these facts on the board, offer a quick explanation, and then point out that students have the time to realize these benefits every day during reading time.

- Tell students to show their book covers to their elbow partners. This activity encourages students to get their books out quickly, introduces a new book to each student, and transitions effortlessly into reading.

- If a few students continue to chat after most of the class is reading, use it as an opportunity to help them mature just a little: Walk over to them, ask them to notice how most of the students in the class are now reading, and

ask them kindly to start reading so they are not inter-
rupting their peers.

These strategies help to create an atmosphere that nurtures
readers. When they have a consistent routine it doesn't take students
long to understand that reading time is a valuable and enjoyable
part of class. It's not a punishment or a drudge, it's an opportunity
for learning, for enjoyment, for self-improvement, for quiet contem-
plation, and it's an activity that everyone joins in together.

Step 5: Model sustained reading in front of your class.

Many students will never have witnessed an adult reading for any
length of time. They're savvy enough to recognize that some adults
claim to value reading but actually don't read very much themselves.
If we want students to attach importance to reading, we must prove
that we truly value it by modeling the behaviors we want them to
adopt. At the beginning of the year I stand directly in front of the
classroom with my current read and spend much of the allotted
reading time immersed in my book. This modeling prompts kids to
take out their books and begin reading more quickly, and they're
more likely to stay on task. The visual reminder that we spend our
class time in sustained reading certainly works better than telling
kids "be quiet" or "start reading."

Step 6: Conduct short reading conferences.

Once you've built momentum with short reading sessions, lengthen
the duration by a few minutes and begin conducting short reading
conferences with individuals. For a class of average size, you will
confer with only a fraction of the students each day, but these

check-ins will become the heart of the support you give students in their reading. Start by choosing 2 to 4 kids each day and simply asking each of them, "How's it going?"

Listen carefully to their answers so you can determine areas of strength and weakness for more intensive conversations later on. With some classes, I can begin short reading conferences a few days into the school year; others require more active monitoring during reading time. Sometimes I alternate reading conferences with modeling my own reading behaviors. Let your knowledge about your students guide your decisions as you move through the steps in this process.

OVERCOMING PUSHBACK

Reluctant readers will derail reading time. If a few of your students seem determined not to read, try to identify with the reasons for their reluctance. For some students, reading is the hardest academic task they will do all day. Do you hate math? If so, consider how you would react if a teacher wanted you to spend time every day doing math for fun. Before you could enjoy it, you'd probably have to find a type of math problem that was at an appropriate level of difficulty for you. People, especially boys, tend to avoid activities if they believe they are not going to be successful. You might be more willing to do some more difficult math problems if they were for an authentic purpose. Let's say you were getting new carpeting for your house and you had to calculate the square footage of the floor. Even if you hate math, you would be likely to persist through difficulty if you could find a valuable purpose for your work.

Reluctant readers often believe there's no real value in reading, perceiving it to be a waste of their time, particularly if they see no improvement in their skills or if they've been forced to read books that are too difficult or do not interest them. Invest some time with these children to find out what interests and passions move them. Seek out books that are at an appropriate reading level *and* feel relevant to the student's life. For some kids, this may mean relaxing your ideas of what is an "appropriate" grade level read until you can hook them into reading. If students are so passionate about dirt biking or gaming or carpentry or a pop star that they will at least read magazine articles about that one topic, begin there and lead them into more complex texts as the year progresses.

Resist the urge to throw kids into a long reading session right away, thinking that more time will lead to better results.

Student Story:

You might need to reconsider your idea of what counts as reading. I had a student—I'll call him Kyle—who was a seriously reluctant reader. I tried throughout the school year to help him find full-length novels and nonfiction books that he might enjoy. By early spring he still had not finished his first book, but he was making more progress than he had up to that time. This happened, at least partially, because I temporarily abandoned the quest to have Kyle read a full-length book. Instead I focused on engaging him in meaningful conversations about any content that he and I could both consume.

He wrote a paper about steroids, so I recommended a documentary called *Bigger, Faster, Stronger* to him. He watched it (I had to hide my joy when he told me so), and I drew on the similarities between reading and viewing to have a conversation with him about the film and its big ideas. He loved technology and rap music, so I selected articles on Snapchat about the evolution of rap lyrics and presented them to him during reading time. Afterwards, we discussed them. He was finally engaged because he enjoyed consuming this information and discussing it with another person. Recognizing that he also liked love stories, I recommended *The Fault in Our Stars* to him, and he began to read it during class. Sometimes taking a step backward in a student's reading may actually be a patient movement toward long-term progress.

Class time is precious. The premise of this book is that nothing—nothing—you can do for your students is more valuable than developing them into lifelong readers, and so setting reading time as a priority in your class is essential. Having said that, some teachers may have concerns about students who do not take the time seriously or who waste time in transitions between reading and other activities. If this is the case, set a timer. Although the idea of timing your reading period may seem unnecessary, it can be a valuable strategy to build momentum and efficiency in your culture of reading. At first, students may be less inclined to read and may even be resistant to your whole plan. By setting a timer, keeping the time limit short, and consistently stopping the reading time only when the timer goes off, you'll gradually get students used to the quiet time set aside for reading every day.

Once students are on board and reading time is an established part of the class routine, you can lengthen the amount of reading time and perhaps eliminate the timer altogether. Another option is to situate the timer so that only you can see it. This prevents reluctant readers from staring at the clock instead of reading. You'll also find that the time goes by quickly if you get immersed in your own reading or conferences, so the timer serves as a reminder to move on to the next portion of your lesson. Eventually, the class will move efficiently into and out of reading period with very little lag time.

If you have concerns that this precious reading time will cut into your ability to cover content, revisit your instructional objectives and set priorities. Compare the importance of each objective to the amount of time you typically devote to it. For example, if you do a mini-lesson on a literary device, consider whether the lesson is as efficient as it can be. Do the students need modeling, guided practice, whole-class review, independent practice, and a closure activity, or will fewer steps suffice?

Students will want more reading time. Of course you can give students as much reading time as you find appropriate. Remember, though, that the students who are begging for more time to read may be a minority. Even though many of your readers may be ready to read for extended periods, having too much time to read could derail others. Resist the urge to throw kids into a long reading session right away, thinking that more time will lead to better results.

Stick to your short, daily practice, and nurture students' reading during that time with one-on-one conversations.

Check in with a few students each day, concentrating especially on the students who are not yet fully engaged. Evaluate their level of frustration and try to determine its source: If they are being held back by lack of reading ability, focus your conversations on helpful strategies and perhaps on finding more appropriate texts. If they've not yet found a book that they like, work some teacher magic and offer them books that you know will grab them. Maintaining connections with reluctant readers throughout the year will lead you to help more students break through their negative self-images as readers and hook into reading. Nothing will make your teacher's heart sing like the day one of your resistant readers is the one to request more time to read.

THE HACK IN ACTION

Jori Krulder, English teacher at Paradise High School in Northern California, knows how to build momentum for the culture of reading in her classroom. It took a shift in perspective on the way she approached reading in her class to make the experience authentic and get kids to fall in love with books.

She had already established a classroom reading routine that was working to some degree: "On Fridays, everybody would bring in books of their choice and we'd do little traditional things with them, you know, every six weeks a book report…It was okay," Krulder says of her initial approach to independent reading. She'd reach one or two kids every year through this system because of her own passion: Her book talks and read-alouds got kids interested in reading.

Her perspective shifted when a professional development book prompted her to compare her efforts to promote reading in her classroom and the way that the adult readers behave: "It wasn't until I read Donalyn Miller's *The Book Whisperer* that I realized the way I was doing it wasn't authentic. People don't read once a week for an hour."

If Krulder had just wanted the kids to be quiet and read, she would've accepted the status quo in her classroom. She had reached a point where her students were compliant: They sat quietly during reading time with their books out on their desks, most of them reading consistently. Once she learned about Donalyn Miller's model, though, compliance no longer felt sufficient. She made a significant change in her approach and established a daily 10- to 15-minute reading practice. For her, the shift felt momentous: "It doesn't sound revolutionary, but it really was, because nobody did it that way."

This reading revolution included a decision to nurture students' identities as readers: "I took away a lot of the requirements. I don't have them do book logs. The only accountability I have for them is that as they're reading I'll walk around and check them off. And for some of them, the ones I know struggle with reading, I'll write down the page number they're on, and I'll talk to them about what they're reading." She helps students find other books to read when they're stuck and addresses individual students' needs as she monitors the classroom during reading time.

She starts the year with a few activities that help to build the momentum of the reading culture in her classroom. Students take a survey that provides them with their first opportunity for self-assessment:

- How many books are in your house?

- What do you think about your STAR reading level?
  (STAR is an adaptive, computer reading test.)

  - Where would you estimate it?

  - How do you feel about that?

  - Where would you like it to be?

- What kinds of reading habits do you have right now?

The survey helps students to think of themselves as readers and establish their reading identities. And by having students set goals, it builds motivation to read: "Their goals were so much less apathetic than it might seem on the surface. They really want to improve. They've been dealing with failure year after year, and have accepted it as part of their image."

Her students tend toward low reading levels and poor self-images, so Krulder starts building class reading culture with the most basic of reading tasks: how to pick a book. "We do something called reading speed dating. You go into the library, where multiple tables have been set up with a bunch of high-interest books. Students go to each table and very quickly peruse each book, look at the back, read a couple pages, and write down books that they're interested in."

Because she knows that some students need additional motivation, Krulder spends time with them to highlight reasons to read. "We read articles every Friday. We spend 10-20 minutes reading and discussing an article on the benefits of reading. Stuff like, 'Ten Reasons You Should Read to Your Child.' Just different things to explain the purpose of reading instead of me just standing up there and saying 'This is good for you,' which they've heard all of their lives."

The fundamental part of this hack is Krulder's interactions with her students about their reading practices. When the bell rings, students get out their books and get started, and Krulder walks around to check in with each student.

She says this shift has increased the number of students who find books they like. And the results have also manifested in improved reading test scores. Despite some ambiguity about the validity of electronic reading tests, for Krulder it is important to be able to show these positive results to students. The upward movement of the data builds momentum because students take pride in their improvement: "There has been a lot more conversation and excitement over reading." As a way to make these results more meaningful, Krulder asks students to reflect on their performance at various points throughout the year and measure these results against their habits as readers.

She tells the story of one boy, Bryce, who said he had never read a book. She convinced him to begin by reading a "tiny little book" about a former gang member. He then moved on to Dave Pelzer's *A Child Called It* series. After finishing his latest reads, Bryce was at a sticking point. He was having trouble finding his next book, and wasn't keeping the momentum going with his independent reading. There was no doubt that he would surmount this obstacle if Krulder had anything to do with it. She makes it a personal challenge to help these reluctant readers get back on track. Her attitude is clear: "I'm relentless."

A culture of readers doesn't build itself overnight. Teachers have to invest time in getting to know students and helping each student find his or her path into daily reading before anything else can happen. Focus on the readers in your classroom first and foremost, and build momentum by gradually devoting class time to reading.

HACK 2

ADAPT READING CULTURE TO FIT CURRICULUM

Adapt yourself to the things among
which your lot has been cast.

—Marcus Aurelius, Roman Emperor/Stoic Philosopher

THE PROBLEM: FITTING INDEPENDENT READING INTO EXISTING CURRICULUM

MANY TEACHERS WORK in environments that allow them only limited autonomy. Considering the prevalence of standards movements and predesigned curriculum packages, educators often end up following curriculum, pacing guides, and daily lesson plans that someone else created. This *someone else* often knows little about the needs of the students sitting in front of you. This *someone else* might not recognize the power of hacking literacy through building a culture of reading.

You might have had a list of assigned texts that students are required to "get through" bestowed upon you. Much of the classic literature typically taught in an English language arts classroom deserves attention and can lead to awesome literacy experiences for students. However, too often these texts fill the entire curriculum, leaving little room for anything else. The combination of required texts and limited time often leads to one of the grand farces of modern American education: Teachers assign a book that they know many students fake their way through with SparkNotes, movies, or cheating strategies, and yet teachers forge ahead with the same plan year after year.

Many of the reading, writing, and speaking skills that form the basis of any literature class or reading and writing workshop can be reinforced through self-selected texts.

Nearly every classroom teacher experiences the challenge of limited class time and expanding curricular demands. Every day feels a little too rushed, every year a little too jam-packed with curriculum. As a result, teachers who are required to teach specific skills and standards may argue that it is simply too difficult to introduce, instruct, and assess standards effectively unless all their students read the same text. Giving students class time to read independently seems impossible with all that teachers are asked to do during the course of the year.

THE HACK: ADAPT READING CULTURE TO FIT CURRICULUM

Curriculum requirements can present a challenge for teachers who want to build a culture of reading in their classrooms. When you face a long list of whole-class texts, standards, and assignments that you are mandated to teach, integrating independent reading into your days might feel unmanageable. However, when authentic learning rather than curriculum coverage takes priority, the benefits of daily reading become obvious. Many of the reading, writing, and speaking skills that form the basis of any literature class or reading and writing workshop can be reinforced through self-selected texts.

Teachers know that one-size-fits-all approaches rarely work, and the inherent diversity of daily independent reading lends itself to differentiating curricular outcomes for individual students. Determine the objectives you have for your class, whether they are to get students to understand specific reading strategies, literary elements, or ways of responding to a text, and give students opportunities to practice meeting the standards with their self-selected reading. Using independent reading as a vehicle to teach curricular outcomes allows you to balance the culture of reading in your classroom with your school's mandated curriculum.

WHAT YOU CAN DO TOMORROW

- **Read lists of book recommendations.** Whether you teach AP Literature or first-grade reading, experts have curated lists of the best books for the level and age of the students you teach. Find a few appropriate lists and compare them to the books you have in your classroom library and the books that students have been bringing to class. While I don't recommend strictly limiting students' reading choices to pre-defined lists, stakeholders like principals and supervisors are often more supportive of integrating choice reading as part of the curriculum if you can provide evidence that students are reading books recommended for their level. Seek out Newbery Medal winners and honor books, the books recommended by the College Board for AP students, the School Library Journal list of best books for the middle grades, and the American Library Association's best books for young adults.

- **Use reading as a basis for quick writes.** A quick write is exactly what it sounds like: a one- to five-minute burst of writing where students are given a prompt, picture, or text to which they respond as quickly as they can without stopping to edit or revise. When students are all reading their own books, you can use quick writes as a way to reinforce writing outcomes in just a few minutes. To build competency in 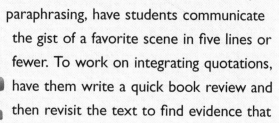 paraphrasing, have students communicate the gist of a favorite scene in five lines or fewer. To work on integrating quotations, have them write a quick book review and then revisit the text to find evidence that

supports their opinions. Boost narrative
writing skills by writing a scene from
a different character's perspective or
rewriting the ending of the book.

- **Conduct a research rally.** Try a research
  rally in class tomorrow to provide your students with
  choices for nonfiction reading. Give students a short
  period of time, I suggest 10 minutes, during which
  they search for articles that relate thematically to
  some element of your curriculum. Bring students to a
  computer lab, allow students to use their own devices
  to search the web, or simply pick up a few copies of
  the newspaper on the way to school and ask students
  to peruse them for relevant articles. There is no need
  to spend an exorbitant amount of money on newspa-
  pers—just create small groups and have students split
  one copy of the paper up between them.

  After the 10 minutes are up, students read one
  of their selected articles, and then plan an elevator
  pitch. The elevator pitch is a very brief presentation—approximately the amount of time you'd
  have to persuade an important person to buy your
  product during an elevator ride. In this case, students
  "sell" their explanation of how the article they found
  connects to the curriculum.

A BLUEPRINT FOR FULL IMPLEMENTATION

Step 1: Use conferences to make curriculum connections.

Set a goal to confer each day with a set number of students or one small group of students about their current books. Use these conferences to introduce, practice, and assess curriculum-related skills. If the class has been tackling a certain skill using shared texts, check in with particular students during conferences and have them apply the skill to their independent reads. For example, if the whole class has been learning how to analyze imagery, have students identify examples of imagery in the books they are reading independently. If you are conducting small group conferences, have the students share these examples with other students in the group.

Step 2: Develop an independent reading project related to the curriculum.

Long-term projects gain new energy when students are able to choose the books they will work on. The exact scope of the project will depend on your curriculum and grade level. As an example, I compiled a list of young adult novels that touch on the topic of diversity for our freshmen "Someone Else's Story" project. The curriculum required that freshmen learn to develop an annotated bibliography and demonstrate public speaking skills with a presentation.

Each student selected one of the novels, chose a character that represented diversity, and generated a research question about some aspect of the character's life. The students researched answers to this question, generating an annotated bibliography of the sources they found. Each of them presented an analysis of his or her chosen book, synthesizing the findings from research to answer the essential question: *What do we learn from reading someone else's story?* The requirements of the curriculum became a framework that deepened our class culture of reading. I used the project to conduct a book pass with the list of diverse books I had selected from the library, to give students daily time to read and confer with me, and to have them give an Ignite-style talk on the book to the class.

Step 3: Plan book club discussions around related readings.

Look for patterns in your students' independent reading selections; develop lists of books that have a similar genre, theme, author, time period, or other characteristic; and organize book club-style discussions based on these patterns and similarities. For example, my colleague noticed a trend among her freshmen: They loved dystopian fiction. For the end of the year, she compiled a list of great dystopian novels, had students select one to read independently, then organized discussions about thematic questions like: *How do humans act when they are desperate? What are the definitions of good and evil? What will our society look like in 50 years?* Another way to build book discussions is to compile lists of texts that complement existing curricular texts. If you are required to teach *The Scarlet Letter*, you can compile a list of young adult books that relate to *The Scarlet Letter* based on a character being ostracized, the genre of historical fiction, or a theme like the struggle to determine morality.

Step 4: Reinforce skills with student-chosen texts.

Teachers often use whole-class texts to teach specific reading strategies or skills that are mandated in the curriculum. Use the texts that students have chosen in order to provide opportunities for more practice of these strategies and skills. You might plan to analyze an author's use of word choice, structure, or perspective; you might have students examine character, setting, or theme; you might teach how to look for arguments and evidence in informational texts. Begin by using one- to two-page texts as the foundation for mini-lessons that will teach these skills. Students can then go on to practice the skill using whatever book they are currently reading, or you may give them excerpts for practice if the skill does not apply readily to a student's book of choice.

If there is a certain skill or strategy that the class will focus on for a sustained period of time, you might provide students with lists of books that offer clear opportunities to practice the skill or strategy. For example, when it was time for my students to practice analyzing point of view in literature, we read excerpts from Cammie McGovern's *Say What You Will*, which features characters with mental or physical disabilities. We read, discussed, and wrote about the points of view in these excerpts as a whole class. Simultaneously, my students were reading books they had selected from a long list featuring characters with diverse perspectives. They each wrote a response that analyzed the characters in his or her book of choice. This allowed me to teach the skill of analyzing perspective to the whole class while also giving students choice in their reading.

OVERCOMING PUSHBACK

There's not enough time to do it all. This hack works efficiency into your daily routine. By beginning with independent reading, you provide a routine that engages kids in literacy as soon as the bell rings and also calms and focuses them for the rest of the period. When you relate curriculum to books students choose to read and practice curricular skills with independent reads, students still reach the learning objectives that you are required to teach. You are simply giving them ownership of some of the reading material they use to practice their learning. This will likely lead to more engagement with the work and better results.

I can't track 25 readers with 25 different books. Making in-class reading a consistent part of the class routine is the best hack I've found to manage this situation. The key to keeping the system manageable is connecting with your students. When you have daily conferences with students, you'll learn about them as individual readers. The more they write and speak to each other about their reading and do curriculum-related work with their independent reading books, the more you'll become immersed in your students' reading lives. You'll develop a sense of what kind of books your individual students like, where they are in their reading progress, and even how often they are reading outside of class. It is amazing what daily conferences can accomplish, even when they are limited to speaking to a few students during the first 10 to 15 minutes of class. They are invaluable in teaching you about your students' reading choices and abilities as well as in tracking.

If you're concerned about keeping accurate records, know that you do not need to track every detail of your students' reading. As with writing, teachers simply do not have the time to assess as much reading as students need to complete if they are to show significant improvement. If the choice is between having students read more or being able to track more, the reading is clearly more important. If a student finishes a book but you did not get to see her write about it or confer with him about it, that is okay. Trust that the consistent practice of daily student reading outlined here will build a culture of readers and make independent reading work with your curriculum. Having students think, speak, and write about their reading is more important than having a perfect system where every detail is tracked, recorded, and assessed.

We need to prepare for the big tests. An often-cited report by Cunningham and Stanovich, "What Reading Does for the Mind," indicates that students who read just 20 minutes per day generally score in the 90th percentile on standardized tests. Giving students even half that time, 10 minutes per day, plus supporting them and building their love of reading, produces a cumulative effect that will help them become better readers. It will also allow for success on the one yardstick that matters to some of the people in power—standardized tests.

Some skills only apply to fiction (or nonfiction). There are few literary elements or reading skills that apply exclusively to either fiction or nonfiction. If a student is reading a book that feels far removed from the skill students are practicing in a mini-lesson, you might consider pre-selecting a passage of suitable length from a book that you know is rich with the literary elements or opportunities for skill practice in which the rest of the class is engaged. Another approach to avoid this situation is to provide students with lists of recommended books that fit the skills or content you will be teaching in your curriculum. This limits choice but ensures that students will be reading books that relate to the skills you are teaching.

THE HACK IN ACTION

Sarah Soper is an English teacher and department chair at Northwest High School in Michigan. Sarah has built a culture of readers across the whole spectrum of high school students: Everyone from her freshmen students to her AP Literature students reads self-selected texts. She shows that curriculum is not an obstacle but an opportunity in building a culture of reading.

Sarah adapts her independent reading program depending on her class. Her AP students choose books from the list provided for AP Literature. Their reading blends two purposes: building a culture of reading and preparing to pass the AP exam. At the end of each trimester, Sarah's AP students each do a project about a book that they've read. The project requires them to analyze the novel they have read using the skills they've learned and practiced in class: analyzing theme, purpose, character, and style.

In Sarah's accelerated ninth-grade class, she takes an integrated approach to independent reading, writing, and speaking to build reading culture while improving literacy skills. Students read Monday, Wednesday, and Friday. She supports students' reading by asking them to reflect in their journals after each reading session. They write about some aspect of their books, connecting the books to skills they have learned and practiced in class. The students then share their journals in small discussion sessions.

With her regular ninth-grade class, Sarah uses a more open-ended approach to building a culture of reading. On Monday, Wednesday, and Friday, students do a skills-related warmup and then have time to read. These students don't do a project at the end of each trimester.

Sarah explains the different approaches for her classes, saying "I want advanced students to get into the literary elements a little bit more, and that's something that will prepare them for Advanced Placement." For her regular ninth graders, "I want it to be low risk. I want them to enjoy reading more, so that's why I give them the time to read. I want them to have fun reading."

When Sarah began reading with her freshmen, many students reported that they were not readers and didn't want to read. Now, they beg for more time to read. Their shift in attitude shows at the end of trimesters, when students ask if they can keep their books after the course has ended so they can finish reading.

"My students are excited to read and they are engaged in reading," Sarah says.

The lesson from Mrs. Soper's class is clear: Regardless of the grade level or curriculum you teach, you can build a culture of reading in your class.

Building a culture of readers in your classroom means adapting to your situation, regardless of the students, class level, or curriculum with which you currently find yourself. Decide on clear objectives for the content and skills you want to teach your students so that you can adapt your culture of reading to support the curriculum instead of taking time away from it.

HACK 3

DEVELOP A
CLASSROOM LIBRARY

*Whatever the cost of our libraries, the price is
cheap compared to that of an ignorant nation.*

—WALTER CRONKITE, BROADCAST JOURNALIST

THE PROBLEM: STUDENTS NEED ACCESS TO BOOKS

MANY STUDENTS ARE not naturally inclined to seek out books. They will eventually learn how to find books that appeal to them with your support if you model the habits and behaviors of a committed reader and nurture their latent enjoyment of reading. However, when students first enter your classroom most of them will not be on the hunt for their next great read.

Their apathy toward books is a problem you must surmount if you want to build a culture of reading in your class. If you are to persuade kids to read regularly, you must ensure that each of them has found a book that he or she is motivated to read. Generally, reluctance to read has its roots in one of two problems: lack of reading skills or poor choice of reading matter. If you can tackle the latter, finding the right book for every student, the former will begin to fix itself.

When students do not have access to interesting books they may develop negative associations with reading. Plenty of today's students come from print-poor environments, so their exposure to the outside world is limited to social media or reality TV. If the only printed texts they ever encounter are the old classics their

The classroom library puts reading right in front of students, it eliminates excuses, and it makes reading multiple books more likely.

teachers have dusted off and handed out once a year, these students will probably not develop into passionate readers. While classic novels certainly have a place in classrooms because of their literary value, students often need support to read them due to their limited background knowledge and reading levels. They are not the kinds of books that get most kids excited to read.

This problem appears daunting: Students have negative associations with reading, their families tend not to support reading, and the books they do encounter are irrelevant or too diffi-cult for them. Fortunately, the solution is a truly simple hack.

THE HACK: DEVELOP A CLASSROOM LIBRARY

A well-curated classroom library can be the key to converting indifferent readers into bookworms. Students must have access to interesting, funny, scary, inspiring, sad, and relevant books if they are ever to feel the transformative effects of reading. It's essential for students who have not had many positive experiences with reading to find a book tailored to their own interests if they are to share in the classroom's reading culture. For such a student, having a teacher say, "Here is a book I chose just for you" can be a powerful impetus to participate. A bountiful classroom library gives a teacher the ability to hand a student an engaging book, tell her she can take it home, carry it around, then return it when she's done. This gives the student a positive experience with reading that might never happen otherwise.

If you can engineer enough positive interactions with books, students will eventually learn how to maintain their own reading momentum. Teachers can keep kids on a reading streak more readily when a classroom library has been established. When you notice that someone is finishing a book, line up a recommendation for the next read. Having a selection of books in the room makes getting a new book into that student's hands painless.

For a kid who's just beginning to make tentative steps into a culture of reading, finding a new book could feel overwhelming. It's easier not to read than to muddle through the process of requesting a recommendation, asking for a hall pass, making a trip to the library, and figuring out how to see if the book is available. When you have books readily accessible, it's a matter of simply taking one off the shelf and handing it to the student. The classroom library puts reading right in front of students, it eliminates excuses, and it makes reading multiple books more likely.

WHAT YOU CAN DO TOMORROW

- **Scour your own shelves.** You may have books in your house that you've already read and enjoyed. If you're willing to share them and you think students will be interested in the types of books you like, start here. You can recommend these selections expertly, since you're so familiar with them. As with many things, the hardest part of creating a classroom library is getting started, so seeing some books on the shelf will get your momentum going.

- **Ask your students to build a wish list.** Amazon has a wish list feature that teachers can hack to build their culture of readers. Get the kids to gather a list of books they would like to read that are not presently in the class library. Then, have students share their lists with you via email so you can compile a master list of their choices. Take 10-20 minutes at the beginning or end of class to complete this process. A Google search for "Amazon Help: Create a List" and "Amazon Help: Share Your List" will provide step-by-step instructions that you can share with students. You might also choose to create a class Amazon account. This would allow students to share books to the same list, and you could then focus on adding those books to your classroom library.

- **Call local public libraries.** Public libraries consistently cull their shelves to make room for new books. Sometimes they have sales to raise funds for the library; sometimes they give the books away. You probably won't get the latest young adult novels this way, but there are still treasures to be found.

- **Head to social media.** I'd begin wherever you have the most real-life connections; this is Facebook, most likely. Write a sincere pitch asking people to check their bookshelves and donate to your cause. This strategy helped me expand my classroom library, thanks to my cousin, Dylan. You might even mention the specific kinds of books you'd like to have donated: young adult fiction, high-interest nonfiction, biographies, science fiction, graphic novels, and any other titles that you think your students will like.

- **Make a pitch to your administrators.** You'll need to articulate your purpose for building a classroom library and specify exactly what you need if you want school funding to buy books for your classroom. Write a well-crafted, polite email to the relevant administrator, explaining your goal and the steps you are taking toward building a culture of reading. Do all of the groundwork in advance so that your charitable administrator just has to say yes. Provide a list of the books you are requesting, including the authors, exact titles, and ISBN numbers; research potential price options; check for availability with the book distributor your district uses if that information is available to you.

- **Elicit help from the PTA.** Ask a student to write a letter to your school's PTA. They do fundraising efforts all the time and have money to give. Their support will depend on how you sell the initiative to them. If they are able to give you any funding, no matter how small the amount, have students write thank you notes. Keep them updated with your achievements and  acknowledge their part in that success. This request might become an annual appeal. If they see tangible results and appropriate appreciation, they are more apt to give again, and in larger amounts.

A BLUEPRINT FOR FULL IMPLEMENTATION

Step 1: Raise funds. Your class library needs some funding. Try one or all of these three recommendations for fundraising for books.

1. **Check out grants and donations.** Thanks to the Internet, it is easier than ever to find opportunities for grants and charitable donations to your classroom library. The Book Love Foundation, a project of the dynamic teacher and author, Penny Kittle, gives

away multiple classroom libraries every year. Google the name of the foundation and you'll find plenty of details and instructions. Another option, if you're willing to put in the time, is DonorsChoose.org, a platform that connects classroom teachers with people who want to donate money to a teacher's project. Though there's a significant amount of work to complete in advance of posting a project, a colleague of mine consistently gets her DonorsChoose projects funded and adds to her classroom library.

2. **Look into commercial book clubs.** Some students are willing and able to buy their own books. Scholastic has long offered students the opportunity to purchase books at discount prices. They periodically send a batch of fliers to participating teachers, who then pass them on to students. For every five books a student buys, he or she gets another one free. The teacher also receives a percentage of the take in the form of vouchers for books. A few weeks after you send the order in, one or more boxes of books will arrive—like Christmas— and you can play Santa Claus as you hand out stacks of books and introduce the new books that you ordered for the class library. The anticipation of receiving the books and the opportunity to build excitement about new reading material makes the effort of managing the orders worthwhile. You do need to be willing to take on the administrational matters associated with the orders and handling the money, which may not feel worth it

if only three students in each class take advantage of the program. If you choose to spend your own money, Scholastic offers good deals on books, and with the bonuses your library will increase rapidly.

3. **Set a small budget to purchase the best books.** Many teachers can't resist picking up books they know their students would like to read. As you continue to build a culture of reading with your students, you'll learn which books are growing in popularity. If you're going to spend your own money on books for your classroom library, make these choices really count by purchasing books that you know many students will enjoy.

Step 2: Develop a book tracking system.

There are several ways to do this, so choose the method that works best based on your own style or organization. One simple way to track books is to use a notecard system. Try this 5-step strategy.

1. Create a file of index cards. Write each student's name in large letters on one side of a card.

2. On the other side, write the student's name in small letters at the top. Underneath the name, create three columns called "Title," "Date out," and "Date in."

3. Teach students the process of checking out books: The student comes to you with the book at the beginning or end of class, and you fill in the title and date on the card.

4. Once a student is finished with a book, he or she shows it to you so you can write down the date it was checked back in. Then the student places the book neatly back in the library.

5. Take out the cards and check up on the students periodically. This will alert you if a student has not been reading consistently or if a book has not been returned for a while.

The cards form a record of your class's reading habits. You'll be able to track how many books each child has read and how long each book took to read. You'll also get a sense of which books are going in and out of your library. If you prefer digital options, there are an increasing number of mobile apps that help teachers to scan and track library books.

Step 3: Ditch Dewey Decimal for big ideas.

Individual students might have favorite authors and preferred genres, but I've found that most students enjoy books with similar themes and storylines. Honor their preferences by using a big ideas organization system for your class library. Separate books into piles based on ideas like love, acceptance, isolation, coming of age, character versus society, etc. Make a label for each category and place the books together on a shelf or in a basket. Want to turn this into a teaching opportunity and save yourself some time? Have students consider the library books they've read and ask them for help categorizing the books.

OVERCOMING PUSHBACK

The good news is that creating a classroom library is something you can do quietly and privately in your own room, so you should not get much pushback from others. The bad news is that you may have to overcome your own doubts, since building a classroom library can be a daunting task.

This task is just too big. In a way you are right. It can be a long, slow process to build a quality classroom library, but the key word here is "quality." Having a few books that students love is better than a room full of books that students are indifferent to. This opinion stems from the firsthand experience of receiving many donations of grocery store paperbacks that no student wanted to read. I eventually removed them from the library altogether. If you gather a handful of books that students want to read, they'll fly off the shelves and you'll build anticipation among other students who see those books getting checked out. Aim for quality, not quantity.

> I try not to take it personally if books go missing from my classroom library. Hopefully, whoever took the book needs it more than I, and it speaks to them on some deeper level that they need.
>
> -Kristen Luettchau, High School English Teacher

The books will get lost or stolen. Yes, some books might not be there at the end of the school year. I consider this a double-edged sword because the books that go missing are often the ones about teens dealing with difficult issues. I can't help but think that the student who has taken the book needs it more than I do. A good book tracking system can handle this problem.

Several teachers use my room throughout the day. Communicate to the sharing teacher, and his/her students if possible, that your classroom library is of great importance to you and your students. Explain that students are welcome to check out books using the same book tracking system your students follow. In my experience, the students from other classes who take books from my classroom library are especially appreciative and careful with them. If that doesn't seem to work, you can always use a portable cart to keep your books with you as you travel throughout the day.

THE HACK IN ACTION

Building the classroom library feels like a monumental task to some teachers. But for Kristen Luettchau, a grade nine English teacher in Mount Olive, New Jersey, she had early role models: her own high school English teachers. She explains, "I always loved my teachers' classroom libraries when I was a student, and I remember my 10th-grade English teacher having a particularly great classroom library, full of all kinds of books in varying genres and levels."

When she became a full-time teacher herself, she found a powerful hack for building her capacity as an English teacher and growing her classroom library: The annual National Council for Teachers of English (NCTE) convention. Kristen explains: "Becoming a member of NCTE and attending their annual convention was one of the best professional career moves I ever made."

This was such a powerful experience because the convention allowed her not only to get free copies of books, but to share her own passion for reading with her students: "Going to the exhibit hall at that convention allowed me to broaden my YA passion and become an expert on different YA texts, meeting authors, getting free advanced reader copies of books, and directing that passion back to my students. I create a class calendar each year with pictures of the authors I've met at NCTE to generate discussions with my students, provide them with book recommendations, and encourage them to see that authors are real people who care about their development."

While Kristen has received many advanced reader copies (ARCs) as a way to grow her classroom library, she is also financially smart when putting her own funds toward the library. "I'm a Barnes & Noble member, and every time I have a little extra money or I get a coupon code, I order more books for my classroom."

As another suggestion for how to use the Amazon Wishlist as a tool, she suggests that teachers have students compile their Wishlists early in the year and then share the master list with parents on Back to School or Open House night. Of course, contributing books to a classroom library is not financially possible for every family, but making these lists public will spread the word, and other community members or business owners may contribute to the library.

Kristen shows she understands the importance of her students' culture of reading when she considers the number of books that disappear from her classroom library every year: "I try not to take it personally if books go missing from my classroom library. Hopefully, whoever took the book needs it more than I, and it speaks to them on some deeper level that they need."

If your students are to fall in love with reading, access to terrific books is a necessity. A classroom library increases the chances that your students will happen upon their new favorite books. When you take care to develop a suitable library, your classroom environment communicates the attitude, "This place nurtures readers." Maintaining a classroom library is hard work, but it pays long-term dividends for your culture of reading.

HACK 4

IMPLEMENT ASSESSMENTS THAT BUILD COMMUNITY

If you find yourself on the side of the
majority, it's time to pause and reflect.
—MARK TWAIN, AUTHOR

THE PROBLEM: ASSESSMENTS DISCOURAGE READING

READING ASSESSMENT BECOMES a strictly extrinsic motivator in many classrooms. Teachers reward kids with grades to push them to read or they threaten failure for not reading enough. Conflating assessment with rewards causes student motivation to suffer. It's human nature to take the shortest route to get the reward. When grades are the goal, assessment backfires, resulting in students reading SparkNotes, watching the movie version, asking friends to summarize a book, or simply lying about reading. The last thing educators intend is to endorse lying and cheating, but an assessment system centered only on earning grades and extrinsic rewards encourages these behaviors.

Some teachers might argue that they need traditional assessment practices to keep records and measure student growth. Even if they agree that grades and rewards should not be used to force reading upon kids, they are willing to accept poor assessment practices that are not in the students' best interests for the sake of data. Yes, quizzes, reading logs, and multiple-choice tests provide quantifiable data and are convenient for updating a gradebook, but their efficiency does not mean that they are the best ways to assess learning. Some assessment strategies are intended to offer information to the teacher and nothing more. While these assessments may be well intended, they often work against teachers' efforts to help readers improve, simply because students approach the assessments as games, not as opportunities to deepen their reading experience. While assessment strategies designed for teacher convenience and efficiency might work for some students and teachers in some situations, they are unlikely to foster a love of reading. Few, if any, adult readers judge their performances based on multiple-choice quizzes or record their start and end times to determine fluency or commitment.

If we want to build a culture that inspires students to become lifelong readers, students should mimic the behaviors of real, engaged readers. Teachers can design assessments that yield information about a student's knowledge and ability to read a text without killing the reading experience. Not only should teachers avoid assessments that encourage students to game the system, but they can effect assessments that deepen the culture of reading.

THE HACK: IMPLEMENT ASSESSMENTS THAT BUILD COMMUNITY

Effective reading assessments are predicated on determining student response to a text. Teachers need students to share their thinking about and knowledge of a text to measure their understanding. When students show what they know and can do, teachers gain information they can use for further instruction. Responses may take the form of speaking, writing, or another form of representation such as a piece of artwork, a design, or a song to demonstrate understanding of a text.

> Assessment no longer takes place in isolation; rather, the social nature of genuinely sharing thoughts about books creates an aspect of social accountability and normalcy to reading and finishing books.

The first step in implementing assessments that build community is to create assessment opportunities that are intrinsically valuable to students. Students feel that an activity has inherent value when they communicate with their classmates about topics or texts that interest them and when they exercise their creativity to make interesting things. Students genuinely want to create quality responses when they communicate their experiences of a text to a real audience.

To develop meaningful assessments, seek real-world models. You might begin by listing the behaviors a typical reader might exhibit outside the classroom. This list will become the basis for a system of authentic assessments. An engaged reader might:

- Listen to a friend's recommendations to evaluate the book's suitability.

- Read reviews on Goodreads or another social media platform.

- Participate in discussions with other readers, addressing a book's ambiguities, interesting moments, character motivations, or the author's style.

- Rate the book and write a review. This might be published on Goodreads, Amazon, a blog, or recorded in a private list of books.

- Write to reflect on the reading experience, document observations about the content, and recommend it to certain types of readers. This might be published on a shared or personal blog.

- Tell friends about the book to persuade them of its quality or to inform them of its content.

flip grid

Teachers will find the items on this list valuable as they facilitate a culture of reading in their classrooms. Rather than simply being a measure of compliance, these activities deepen the reading experience for students, encouraging them to fashion strong identities as readers. They also provide valuable information about a student's ability and knowledge, both during and after the reading process.

The benefit of this sort of activity to assess reading lies not only in the students' authentic motivation to excel, but in building the community of readers. The student audience benefits from the work of their peers as they model personal and critical responses to texts. They see real-life exemplars sharing thoughts about texts in both formal and informal contexts.

The interactions between readers offer opportunities for evaluation, both with regard to the quality of student work and whether the text under consideration appeals to personal reading preferences. Integrating the process of assessment into the everyday work of the classroom in this way forges connections between students and establishes the classroom as a community of readers. Assessment no longer takes place in isolation; rather, the social nature of genuinely sharing thoughts about books creates an aspect of social accountability and normalcy to reading and finishing books. Reading becomes an expectation, an essential aspect of participating in class culture.

Adapting the habits of readers into assessment tools accomplishes two things: Students enjoy a more positive reading experience, and teachers gain insight into meaningful aspects of each student's ability. Unlike multiple-choice quizzes, low-level questioning, and required essays, authentic assessments will inspire students to read more instead of relying on tricks and deception to earn grades without reading.

WHAT YOU CAN DO TOMORROW

- **Introduce the three-sentence book talk.** For some students, their two biggest fears are combined in the book talk: reading and public speaking. I don't expect students to have a natural feel for talking about books because many of them have never observed literate adults discussing their reading. Compound uncertainty about what to say with speaking in front of the whole class, and traditional oral book reports can be a real torment for students. I model book talks often, especially at the beginning of the school year, so students grasp their intent and substance. Later in the fall, as students are finishing their own books, I hand over the opportunity to conduct book talks to them. The three-sentence book talk scaffolds their performances and waylays anxiety. Have the students share the answers to these three questions in one sentence each:

- What's the gist of your book's plot?
- Why did you like it or dislike it?
- Who else should read the book?

These questions allow a student to demonstrate literal understanding; to reflect on the plot, genre, and style; to evaluate a text's appeal to an audience.

The clear beginning and ending, the concise format, and the limited content make this initial oral presentation manageable for most students. The opportunity for students to publicly share their reading requires them to identify as readers, which may be a

first for many middle or high school students. For the teacher, the book talk provides a quick glimpse into a student's level of understanding and depth of thought. The student audience hears about a book they might want to read.

- **Build a quotation wall.** Give each student a sticky note or a small piece of paper and some clear tape. Ask them to write the title of the book they are reading and a favorite line on one side of the paper. Encourage them to *hear* the author's words and to look for lines that sound great when read aloud. This focus will prompt kids to notice aspects of an author's style that they might otherwise ignore. On the back side of the note, they should write one to two sentences justifying the reasons they selected the quotation. Stick the notes on a dedicated wall so you can assess students' understanding through their selection of and responses to quotations, and so students can access reading recommendations.

A BLUEPRINT FOR FULL IMPLEMENTATION

Step 1: Create big idea books.

Penny Kittle discusses this twist on journaling in *Book Love*. Big idea books act as a useful assessment tool for teachers, a valuable way to deepen thinking about reading for students, and a compilation of student contributions to your classroom reading culture.

Collect some simple blank notebooks. Those with a solid-colored cover work best. Label the cover of each notebook with a thematic concept about literature. Consider using ideas like "identity," "alienation," "survival," and "character versus society", themes that apply to many of the books your students will read. Each student will choose a notebook with the idea that pertains to the novel he or she is currently reading. Students write to explain how the big idea connects with the novel.

A variety of approaches to the big idea books could be effective, depending on your goals. You might have everyone write for 15 minutes on Tuesdays, individual students might have the option to write in a notebook one day a week instead of reading, or students might pick up a notebook if they've finished classwork. Students can choose whether or not to sign their names on the entry, but make sure they record the page number, date, and book title so you can assess their writing and ideas.

The real impact of the big idea books stems from the fact that they belong to the classroom and not to individual students. They exist to be shared between students, classes, and school years, so current students will be interacting in writing with future students, and a student in one class can read the entry of a student in a different class to determine whether a novel she mentions would be a good reading choice for him. The big idea books will become precious archives of your students' thinking and also a record of all of the great books that they have read in your class.

Step 2: Increase the expectations for book talks.

After my students gain comfort by presenting a three-sentence book talk, I extend the requirements of the book talk and use it as an opportunity to practice and assess public speaking skills. Students can speak for one minute, or whatever time you deem appropriate. Give kids a defined structure for their book talks, or give them more freedom, depending on their comfort levels. I use Erik Palmer's PVLEGS heuristic for teaching and assessing public speaking. Palmer suggests that students be instructed and assessed on poise, voice, life, eye contact, gestures, and speed. These longer book talks provide me with information about which aspects of public speaking students need to practice. The focus on presentation builds student confidence and skill so that their book talks tend to be of higher quality. The student audience responds to the speakers' increased efficacy, and so the book recommendations with which they are presented almost daily often persuade individual students to seek out new books to read.

Step 3: Ditch the book reports and craft book reviews.

Book reports have been a traditional way to assess reading, but their value to an authentic culture of reading is limited. Teach students instead to write book reviews using mentor texts from sites like *The New York Times* for more advanced students, and *YA Love Blog* for younger students. After students write their reviews, they can print them, mount them on construction or other decorative paper, and display them next to the book. Thus, the reviews serve as written evidence of students' reading as well as providing recommendations to other students.

Step 4: Introduce student-designed assessments.

Guide students with effective scaffolding throughout the year and eventually they'll be competent enough to create and complete their own reading assessments. Set the purpose for the students: The products they develop should demonstrate that they have read and understood their books. If you wish, you can establish criteria for success, or have the class co-construct the criteria. In either case, clearly articulate what success looks like using specific details: Do they address character? Plot? Theme? Author's style? You might determine that the assessment requires a writing component or an oral presentation. If your department, school, or district leaders mandate a certain number or type of reading assessments, allowing students the freedom to design and implement their own assessments can provide creativity and balance.

OVERCOMING PUSHBACK

Assessment is a hot-button issue in education, and it is likely that school leaders and colleagues will point to assessment when critiquing non-traditional reading instruction. Prepare yourself accordingly.

These assessments don't provide the right data. When you assess students authentically they develop a body of work that adequately depicts their progress in reading, writing, and speaking. Of course, the students and the teacher are responsible for keeping track of this work so growth can be monitored over time. Concrete evidence from student work will counter the misconception that moving away from traditional assessment means that teachers just leave student progress up to chance. Appraising several pieces written in response to reading at various points in the school year will demonstrate conclusively that a student's thinking and writing have become increasingly sophisticated.

Combine this evidence with your anecdotal notes about conferences, records of book talks, and student self-evaluations, and you'll easily justify your assessment practices. Compare this data to a set of numbers in a gradebook. Whereas you might see a number average that has steadily risen throughout the year, there is no sense of what that number average represents. If a traditional test like Accelerated Reader or standardized reading test is required at some point during the year, then it is better to use it as one snapshot of student performance in a series of assessments that provide data about student learning.

I can't keep track of all that evidence. Digital tools now make collecting data easier than ever. My students keep all their work in Google Drive. Even if the students write on paper, as with the big idea books, or record audio of themselves talking about a novel, they take pictures, share links, or upload files of their work into Google Drive. The accumulated documents create a portfolio that accurately traces where students began and where they ended up. There's no need to interpret multiple-choice quizzes or even to analyze rubrics closely, because the portfolio of work is right there for all stakeholders to see.

Students need to know where they stand in the class. Feedback is the other essential piece of this assessment process. When you replace quizzes and tests with frequent opportunities for speaking and writing, you don't stop reporting to students, parents, and administrators about student performance. Good assessment practices necessitate providing specific, targeted feedback about strengths and weaknesses that students can use to revise their work or to improve on future work. Keeping stakeholders apprised of student performance involves more than simply providing a number or letter grade.

Some teachers might believe that authentic assessment somehow excuses them from entering data into an online gradebook. I would advocate for using the online gradebook frequently to report on student progress with written commentary. Pairing a portfolio of student products with a consistent record of feedback provides a balanced account of student progress. Students, parents, and administrators can all determine a student's literacy skills by examining samples of work and the associated descriptive feedback.

These assessments don't prepare kids for the big tests. The most valuable test preparation a teacher can offer is to build students' reading habits. Students who read more perform better on standardized tests. Reading is an investment in children's continued success, as they'll develop vocabulary, comprehension, and stamina, all typically leading to better results on high stakes tests. Building a culture of readers will likely prepare students to do well on standardized tests, whereas focusing on test prep does nothing to promote a culture of readers.

Students must learn how to do literary analysis. I sometimes hear teachers claim that they would love to have students do more authentic assessments, but they do not have time because they must teach formal literary analysis. Their statement implies that when students write and speak for authentic audiences, such as other students, they are not analyzing the text. This is a misconception. Students can offer evidence for their ideas and make thoughtful comments about the author's style, a text's genre, or a novel's theme whether they are presenting a book talk, composing a book review, or writing in a big idea book. The instruction and expectations dictate the level of thinking students will demonstrate to a greater extent than the type of assessment they complete. In fact, when students are passionate about an activity they are more likely to engage in the kind of higher-level thinking that is foundational to literary analysis.

THE HACK IN ACTION

"When you give kids an option, they're able to learn from each other. When you give them that freedom of choice, they'll surprise you with what they can do." These are the words of Gerilyn Lessing, an English language arts teacher at Bay Shore Middle School in Long Island. Gerilyn's students read for the first 10 minutes of every 40-minute class period. She has scrapped reading logs in favor of conferences, journals, and student-created assessments.

"What brought me back to reading workshop was my own son. Last year he got this reading log, and…he just didn't want to read. Even though I was the one filling it out, it killed his desire to read. This year, he came home with it and I said, nicely, 'He reads every single night and we're with him, and that's it.'" Reflecting on her experience with her son's education, Gerilyn created a system where her students authentically demonstrate understanding of their reading any way they can imagine.

The instructions are simple: Turn in something once a week to demonstrate understanding of your reading. "I shouldn't have to make the kids jump through a million hoops to show or prove that they've read," Gerilyn explains. Some students just write a paragraph about their books, while other students complete wildly creative and original projects. "These are things that I never could have come up with. Lots of kids write me letters, things like that."

Some teachers might wonder about the kinds of scaffolding that are necessary for such open-ended assessments. What about the students who are lost without a clear sense of direction?

"I have forms that are available to the students. It's really up to them. They can do any [assignment] they want or they can take advantage of the forms." She has students write using forms that resemble other media—film strips, text chats, Instagram posts—and also more traditional book summaries and character descriptions. "After seeing these forms, then the kids start to come up with their own ideas for what to do. Some of the kids take the idea and they make it their own," Gerilyn explains. "Some kids need more structure, and it's available to them if they need it. Some kids who like to push themselves will invent a new option on their own."

She and her students have collaboratively created a culture where reading is valued. "They love being asked about their books and what they've learned. They know each other's interests: This one loves fantasy books and has read all of the *The Selection* series; this one loves graphic novels. They all know this about each other. This is because they're talking about their books and their work is hanging up." Gerilyn posts student work all over her classroom. "My whole room is covered in their independent reading book stuff: their pictures, their poems, their drawings."

She recognizes that using book talks is an authentic way of assessing students' reading and getting them to engage in conversation about their reading. "Tuesday is for books talks. Thursday is for journal writing. Monday, Wednesday, and Friday I conference with the kids. Some days I read with the kids." The assessments give Gerilyn a clear picture of what her students are reading, too. "I have about 140 students, and I can probably tell you what every single one of them is reading."

She grades them with a check or check plus. "It doesn't matter if there's a grade on the paper for them, they get so much feedback in the conversations from me. They know I value their work."

Proof that Gerilyn has made authentic assessment a part of her culture of reading? The students keep it going even when she is out of the classroom. "I had to go to a meeting one day last week, and the students did the daily book talk *and* took the picture. Even with the sub, they took over the class and they did it."

When your classroom becomes a culture of readers, assessments can enhance students' reading experience instead of ruining it. Design assessments that allow students to respond authentically to their texts and to each other. Provide opportunities for students to use their creativity to demonstrate what they've learned from their reading.

HACK 5

SPOTLIGHT READING IN YOUR SCHOOL

That first follower is what transforms a lone nut into a leader.
— DEREK SIVERS, ENTREPRENEUR

THE PROBLEM: READING CULTURES EXIST IN ISOLATION

THIS CHAPTER DETAILS an important last step that is not as easy as managing your own classroom, but holds equal importance to the goal of hacking literacy.

Transforming students from non-readers to book lovers requires persistence and dedication. Each year as I build momentum for the reading culture in my classroom, I see small victories when students finish their books at home, read more books than they ever have, or discuss their reading choices with classmates. This success motivates me to keep following the process: give book talks, conference with students, help the reluctant reader find the book she will love. While I have confidence that my students' reading skills and enjoyment increase significantly in my class, I worry that their success will get derailed after they leave me.

As the hacks in this book illustrate, the actions required to build a culture of reading are simple, yet they must become habitual if teachers are to create lifelong readers. Literacy instruction reaches its maximum effectiveness when students are part of a culture of readers year after year, and when the whole school participates in a culture of reading. This is the true goal of hacking literacy: making literacy integral to everyday school life so that reading forms an indelible component of students' identities.

One obstacle to initiating school-wide reading culture is that teachers can only control influences in their own classroom environments. Few teachers work in a dual supervisor/teacher role, and many do not have the opportunity to share ideas with their colleagues through professional learning communities or other collaborative work groups. While one teacher is creating a thriving reading culture, another might be teaching students in a reading desert. This difference could be attributed to honest ignorance on the part of the teacher. He may not recognize or be exposed to the practices that foster a culture of reading in the classroom. But this lack of consistency undermines the goal of getting students to make reading part of their school lives and part of their identities.

THE HACK: SPOTLIGHT READING IN YOUR SCHOOL

Promote reading in every way possible beyond the doors of your classroom. Encourage teachers and students to share their reading lives with the school community. Hold events that prompt students to talk with each other and staff about books that they love. Make reading social by sharing meals over book discussions. Organize fun events that offer books as a reward, not a means to some other reward. Celebrate reading publicly; heighten its status to amplify its social acceptability. Make reading a cool thing to do. Integrate positive attitudes to reading and habitual reading practices into your school so that students get immersed in reading culture.

 **WHAT YOU CAN DO TOMORROW**

- **Discuss reading culture with your school librarian.**
  The school library and librarian provide essential support for a school-wide reading culture. Talk to your school librarian about the reading culture that you are building in your classroom and discuss your hope to take the reading culture school-wide. Ask what initiatives the librarian has planned to promote reading and offer to collaborate to make them successful. Perhaps the library has acquired new additions that you can highlight to students and staff. You might promote the library's upcoming events with your students. You may have ideas to make the library a more inviting space for students to come to read. If your librarian seems open to suggestions, share your ideas to make the library a hub of school-wide reading culture. As with any complex

endeavor, this work cannot all be done tomorrow, but initiating dialogue is a positive first step. You will almost certainly find an ally in your quest to strengthen school reading culture.

- **Display your class's reading life on your door.** Exploit kids' natural curiosity about what happens in other classes to spread buzz about books outside your classroom. Ask your students to think of the title of a book that they have recently finished. Show examples of effective blurbs from the back of fiction and nonfiction books so they see how a short statement can capture a reader's feelings about a book. Hand out paper and instruct them to write their names and their book's title and author on the top of the page. Underneath, they write a one-sentence comment that encapsulates their experience with the book. Tape these short book reviews on your classroom door. Now every student in the school can see that your class is full of readers. The reviews will initiate book discussions between students in your class and their peers, and your colleagues will notice the reading culture you are building in your classroom.

- **Share your students' reading success on social media.** If you have a class Twitter, Facebook, Goodreads or other social media account, celebrate your students' reading accomplishments publicly. I started this practice by sharing my students' blog post reviews on Twitter, mentioning the authors of the books my students had reviewed. Your post might include the words, "Maria finished five books this quarter!" with a picture of the books stacked together. These posts do not need to contain pictures of students or their last names (and probably should not). 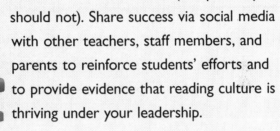 Share success via social media with other teachers, staff members, and parents to reinforce students' efforts and to provide evidence that reading culture is thriving under your leadership.

A BLUEPRINT FOR FULL IMPLEMENTATION

Step 1: Transfer your reading activities to common school spaces.

Colleagues will be more likely to support your efforts at creating a reading revolution in your school if they know exactly what it looks like. Model effective reading culture by moving book talks and book passes to visible spots in the school, like the school library or other common areas. Both staff and students will be intrigued by the activities, presenting opportunities for you to spread the word about reading and possibly opening discussions about effective reading instruction.

Step 2: Share students' reading lives publicly.

One way to spread a culture of reading throughout a school is to provide opportunities for students to share their favorite books with the school community. This establishes reading as a normal activity for students, and can get kids talking to each other about their favorite books. One way to accomplish this is to have students write short reviews of their favorite books, and then post those reviews next to the physical copy of the book in the library. Students see that their writing has an authentic audience, and the library benefits from student book recommendations.

Step 3: Make reading the reward.

Some school-wide reading programs suggest that rewards incentivize students into reading more. Students win a pizza party if they read a certain number of books in a month, or they receive gifts like stickers and pencils for meeting reading accomplishments. Students may read more in the short term in such cases, but once the prizes disappear, so do the books. Rather than implying that only a reward would prompt a kid to read, spark interest in reading for its own sake. Make reading the reward.

Plan a book giveaway activity, where students have fun and receive books as prizes. You might consider a school-wide holiday book exchange, where students bring in a favorite book from home, wrap it up like a gift, then exchange the books in the library or another common area. Giver and recipient then have time to meet and discuss the book. You may decide if the books are kept or returned to their original owners. Rather than handing out certificates for good deeds, academic excellence, or other school honors, present book awards. When adults demonstrate that they consider books valuable by sharing interesting books as rewards, students will be more likely to value books themselves.

Step 4: Hold a "Literature Lunch."

Ask teachers in your school to nominate students to take part in a book club discussion during lunchtime. Choose a high-interest book that all participating students and staff will read by a certain date. Hold the discussion during the school's typical lunch period in a common area like a classroom. If your school has a culinary arts class, you might solicit their help in preparing the lunch. The food need not be special, though; students can eat their own bag lunches or bring food from the school cafeteria. When they participate in a discussion about a book with both staff and students in attendance, student perspectives on reading shift to view reading as lifelong adult readers see it. Reading belongs in all stages of life as a way to expand one's mind and engage in discussions with others about interesting stories and ideas.

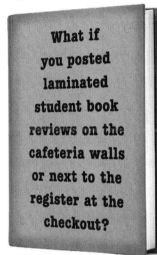

What if you posted laminated student book reviews on the cafeteria walls or next to the register at the checkout?

Step 5: Broadcast reading achievements on school television.

As students finish books, collect their names and the titles that they've read. For each, create an image on a PowerPoint or Google slide with the student's name, the title of the book, and a picture of the cover. Include a caption like, "Jane Doe just finished reading *The Hunger Games*." Ask the audio/video department, or whomever is in charge of the school's closed circuit TV, to broadcast your slideshow whenever other announcements are not displayed.

Students will love seeing their reading accomplishments shared with the school community. Keep reading visible by celebrating student achievement to highlight its cool factor.

Step 6: Invite colleagues to participate in planning and organizing reading celebrations.

For a culture to sustain itself, its common knowledge has to be disseminated amongst all members of the culture. Although a leader can instigate change, others must participate to integrate these changes into the existing culture. Invite other teachers or administrators to hold their own reading celebrations in your school. Start small by asking one teacher to collaborate with you on an event, ask for input on a reading celebration, help someone else plan an activity. Encourage people to plan and implement future reading celebrations in the school. By involving others, you can ensure that the culture of reading in your school will live on into the future.

OVERCOMING PUSHBACK

Reading celebrations disrupt the atmosphere of the library. If noise is the issue, consider conducting a silent book pass in the library, or notify others by posting a sign on the library entrance or sending an email announcing that an activity will take place in the library that might be a little noisy. Be sure to include that all are welcome to participate. If using the library is the problem, invite teachers into your room to see how you do book passes and book talks, or perhaps conduct them in the hallway with students sitting on the floor.

The librarian is not interested in posting class projects. If the school librarian rejects your request to collaborate on a project like placing book reviews next to the books in the library, consider other alternatives. Brainstorm how you might display students' responses to their reading in other physical or digital spaces. What if each administrative office featured a hardcover copy of a book and a student's book review? What if you posted laminated student book reviews on the cafeteria walls or next to the register at the checkout? Could you create QR codes that link to student work and publish them in the school newspaper?

Others complain about too few or too many attendees. Sparse attendance often results from too little publicity. If, on the other hand, you're overwhelmed by attendees, you may suspect that many of them don't really want to participate in the activity, but have appeared as a way of escaping from class. Both of these issues could be solved through the same process: Ask teachers to nominate students to attend. The limited number of seats available makes the event special, and also gives the teachers the power to nominate students who will enjoy attending the event, approach it maturely, and benefit from it.

We don't have access to television in our school common area. Broadcast your celebrations on paper. Create a celebration wall using a large piece of poster paper or newsprint. Students use colorful markers to sign their names and write the titles of the books they have finished. You could also consider requesting the use of a trophy case or other display showcase to hang a sign displaying students' reading achievements.

THE HACK IN ACTION

This Hack in Action contains two stories, both from my home state of New Jersey. They show how a variety of the strategies shared in this chapter spotlight reading in a school.

Part 1: Amy Gazaleh

Amy Gazaleh, the librarian at Hightstown High School in New Jersey, has brought staff together to share their reading lives and has improved the physical space of the library to promote a culture of reading.

One change Amy made represents her stance toward student reading in a concrete way. She removed alarm sensors near the doors to create a more welcoming space. Previously, an alarm would sound if students left the library with a book that had not been checked out. The removal of the alarms was a philosophical decision about the importance of books in students' lives: "Entering the library by walking through security gates did not generate the message that this is a safe space in which everyone is welcome. I do not believe there is a problem with students stealing books—library books are free, after all—and those few that do steal them need them more than I do," Amy explains.

In addition to making the library a more welcoming space for students to come find books, Amy has promoted the culture of reading by inviting staff to share their reading lives with the school. At the beginning of the 2015-2016 school year, each teacher received a door sign for sharing their current reads. For example, mine says, "Mr. Dawson is reading…" with white space to fill in the title. Amy hopes the signs connect students with staff, and staff with each other: "The goal of the reading signs was to expand the reading conversation beyond the library and English classes. I want students to think about reading as a habit of mind, not an assignment, and to find common ground with someone in the building." Students often check out books from the library and explain to Amy that they discovered the titles from a teacher's door sign. The teachers' selections reveal interests that might not show in the classroom: science teachers read classics, history teachers read sci-fi, language teachers read historical fiction.

Amy has metaphorically blasted open the walls of the library to expand reading culture into the school. She visits classes to present book talks about thematically related texts that teachers have requested or new additions to the school library. For staff who want reading recommendations but struggle to find the time to search the library, Amy sends out a monthly "Book Blast" newsletter containing a list of thematically related books. In partnership with Mrs. Kudish, she has also created a staff book club, which had not previously existed. The idea behind this is simple, yet powerful: Every other month, teachers and administrators meet to discuss a shared book they have read. The books are either young adult fiction or nonfiction that might pique students' interests.

Part 2: Steve Ferguson and Christine Finn

Steve Ferguson is an English teacher at Cedar Creek High School in Egg Harbor City, New Jersey, and Christine Finn is the media specialist at Cedar Creek. Together, they've created a school-wide culture of reading through celebration and communication.

Steve and Christine created the hashtag #PiratesRead on Twitter as a way for students and staff to share conversations about books and communicate with authors. Steve explains that the hashtag was a simple way to build the culture of reading in their school: "The response from the students is positive, especially when they receive responses from the author or the author 'favorites' their tweet," Steve said.

Christine acknowledges the power that social media has for a school that wants to build public perception as a culture of readers. "We might not have the money for an author visit, but we can still give our students the opportunity to make a real world connection with writers. Tweets present doors to open conversations and to share interests which in turn builds rapport."

Steve and Christine have also started "Lit Lunch," a program where students eat lunch together and discuss a shared read. Culinary arts students prepare the lunch, the morning announcements TV show helps advertise the book selections, and teachers recommend the books. The collaboration between these groups helps emphasize the importance and celebration of reading in the school. The group meets for one and a half periods to talk about the book and eat together. Steve has observed diverse student perspectives being shared during Lit Lunches. "At times, it feels like *The Breakfast Club*. In fact, like *The Breakfast Club*, Lit Lunch allowed us to reach students who may not have otherwise found a group within the school community."

Steve and Christine show that giving students opportunities to discuss books, in person or online, extends the culture of reading in a school.

Make the reading in your classroom transparent to everyone else in the school, and then celebrate reading throughout the building. Involve as many of the other students, faculty, and staff as you can. Hold fun events that are centered around reading and talking about books to spread your culture of reading throughout the school.

CONCLUSION
Literacy is the meta-hack

How do you hack learning? By hacking literacy. Literacy is the one hack that is absolutely required to make progress in almost any area of education or in life, for that matter.

When you build a culture of reading in your class and school so students see themselves as readers, they're also becoming better citizens and more effective human beings. People who read learn to look outside their limited personal perspectives: They become curious about other people and the rest of the world. Their reading builds background knowledge that opens them up to new experiences and understanding. Readers want to stay informed because they want to learn about the topics they care about. Teachers who foster a culture of reading also foster a healthy democracy: Their readers are future voters who read up on the issues that matter to them.

Readers are generally more interesting people, too. They've experienced hundreds or thousands of lives based on the characters and narrators they've encountered. Reading is one of the few ways that a person can enter completely into the mindset of another human being without fear or judgment. Empathy results. Their vicarious experiences of other realities may help them develop a moral sense, the ability to deeply consider life's big ideas, a capacity for critical thought. Their reading may therefore enrich relationships with friends, family, coworkers, and total strangers.

I refer to literacy as the meta-hack because it creates a ripple effect that can potentially improve all other areas of a student's academic and personal life. Its impact makes creating a culture of readers of the utmost importance. I'll go so far as to say that if we were to do only one thing in school, if we had to get rid of everything else, we should be helping students to be better, more engaged readers. Reading is the best gift that we can give students to set them up for a successful future.

OTHER BOOKS IN THE HACK LEARNING SERIES

HACKING EDUCATION
10 Quick Fixes For Every School

By Mark Barnes (@markbarnes19) & Jennifer Gonzalez (@cultofpedagogy)

In the bestselling *Hacking Education*, Mark Barnes and Jennifer Gonzalez employ decades of teaching experience and hundreds of discussions with education thought leaders, to show you how to find and hone the quick fixes that every school and classroom need. Using a Hacker's mentality, they provide one Aha moment after another with 10 Quick Fixes For Every School—solutions to everyday problems and teaching methods that any teacher or administrator can implement immediately.

"Barnes and Gonzalez don't just solve problems; they turn teachers into hackers—a transformation that is right on time."

— DON WETTRICK, AUTHOR OF *PURE GENIUS*

MAKE WRITING
5 Teaching Strategies That Turn Writers Workshop Into a Maker Space

By Angela Stockman (@angelastockman)

Everyone's favorite education blogger and writing coach, Angela Stockman, turns teaching strategies and practice upside down in the bestselling, *Make Writing*. She spills you out of your chair, shreds your lined paper, and launches you and your writer's workshop into the maker space! Stockman provides five right-now writing strategies that reinvent instruction and inspire both young and adult writers to express ideas with tools and in ways that have rarely, if ever, been considered. Make Writing is a fast-paced journey inside Stockman's Western New York Young Writer's Studio, alongside the students there who learn how to write and how to make, employing Stockman's unique teaching methods.

"Offering suggestions for using new materials in old ways, thoughtful questions, and specific tips for tinkering and finding new audiences, this refreshing book is inspiring and practical in equal measure."

—AMY LUDWIG VANDERWATER, AUTHOR AND TEACHER

HACKING ASSESSMENT
10 Ways to Go Gradeless in a Traditional Grades School

By Starr Sackstein (@mssackstein)

In the bestselling *Hacking Assessment,* award-winning teacher and world-renowned formative assessment expert Starr Sackstein unravels one of education's oldest mysteries: How to assess learning without grades—even in a school that uses numbers, letters, GPAs, and report cards. While many educators can only muse about the possibility of a world without grades, teachers like Sackstein are reimagining education. In this unique, eagerly anticipated book, Sackstein shows you exactly how to create a remarkable no-grades classroom like hers, a vibrant place where students grow, share, thrive, and become independent learners who never ask, "What's this worth?"

"The beauty of the book is that it is not an empty argument against grades–but rather filled with valuable alternatives that are practical and will help to refocus the classroom on what matters most."

— ADAM BELLOW, WHITE HOUSE PRESIDENTIAL INNOVATION FELLOW

HACKING THE COMMON CORE
10 Strategies for Amazing Learning in a Standardized World

By Michael Fisher (@fisher1000)

In *Hacking the Common Core,* longtime teacher and CCSS specialist Mike Fisher shows you how to bring fun back to learning, with 10 amazing hacks for teaching the Core in all subjects, while engaging students and making learning fun. Fisher's experience and insights help teachers and parents better understand close reading, balancing fiction and nonfiction, using projects with the Core and much more. *Hacking the Common Core* provides read-tonight-implement-tomorrow strategies for teaching the standards in fun and engaging ways, improving teaching and learning for students, parents, and educators.

HACKING LEADERSHIP
10 Ways Great Leaders Inspire Learning That Teachers, Students, and Parents Love

By Joe Sanfelippo (@joesanfelippoFC) and Tony Sinanis (@tonysinanis)

In the runaway bestseller Hacking Leadership, renowned school leaders Joe Sanfelippo and Tony Sinanis bring readers inside schools that few stakeholders have ever seen—places where students not only come first but have a unique voice in teaching and learning. Sanfelippo and Sinanis ignore the bureaucracy that stifles many leaders, focusing instead on building a culture of engagement, transparency and, most important, fun. Hacking Leadership has superintendents, principals, and teacher leaders around the world employing strategies they never before believed possible.

"The authors do a beautiful job of helping leaders focus inward, instead of outward. This is an essential read for leaders who are, or want to lead, learner-centered schools."

—GEORGE COUROS, AUTHOR OF THE INNOVATOR'S MINDSET

HACK LEARNING RESOURCES

All things Hack Learning:

hacklearning.org

The Entire Hack Learning Series on Amazon:

hacklearningbooks.com

The Hack Learning Podcast, hosted by Mark Barnes:

hacklearningpodcast.com

Hack Learning on Twitter

@HackMyLearning

#HackLearning

#HackingLeadership

#HackingLiteracy

#HackingEngagement

#HackingHomework

#HackPBL

#MakeWriting

The Hack Learning Academy:

hacklearningacademy.com

Hack Learning on Facebook:

facebook.com/hacklearningseries

The Hacking Engagement Podcast, hosted by James Sturtevant:

jamesalansturtevant.com

The Hack Learning Store:

hacklearningstore.com

ABOUT THE AUTHOR

 **Gerard Dawson** teaches English and Journalism to students in grades 9-12 at Hightstown High School in New Jersey. Gerard is a contributing author to the Talks With Teachers publication *The Best Lesson Series: Literature,* and his work has appeared in The New York Times Learning Network, Edutopia, and Brilliant or Insane. He believes in technology's power to revolutionize learning and offers a free online course for teachers: "How to Put Feedback First for Student Learning." Gerard lives in New Jersey with his wife, Jennifer, and son, Gerard. Follow him on Twitter @gerarddawson3.

ACKNOWLEDGEMENTS

I'M GRATEFUL THAT Mark Barnes gave me this opportunity and provided help and guidance throughout the process. He's taught me so much about teaching, writing, and sharing a message. A big thank you to all of the educators who spoke to me for the individual chapters of the book, including Kristen Luettchau, Steve Ferguson, Christine Finn, Amy Gazaleh, Jori Krulder, Gerilyn Lessing, and Sarah Soper. Your ideas have all made me a better teacher. I appreciate the time that Kevin Akey, Jim Mahoney, Dr. Emily Meixner, and Dave Stuart Jr. spent providing valuable feedback on initial drafts of the book and all they've done as my educational role models.

Thanks to my Mom and Dad, sister Tara, and the Mosesku family for their love and support. Thanks to my son, Gerard, for showing me when it's time to stop writing and start playing.

And thanks to my wonderful wife, Jen, for keeping her vows and supporting my goals.

PUBLICATIONS

Times 10 is helping all education stakeholders improve every aspect of teaching and learning. We are committed to solving big problems with simple ideas. We bring you content from experts, shared through multiple channels, including books, podcasts, and an array of social networks. Our mantra is simple: Read it today; fix it tomorrow.

Stay in touch with us at #HackLearning on Twitter and on the Hack Learning Facebook page. To work with our authors and consultants, visit our Team page at hacklearning.org.

43155894R00061

Made in the USA
Lexington, KY
25 June 2019